THE HARDY TREE

THE HARDY TREE

LINDA BIERDS

COPPER CANYON PRESS

PORT TOWNSEND, WASHINGTON

Copper Canyon Press is in residence at Fort Worden State Park in Port Townsend, Washington, under the auspices of Centrum. Centrum is a gathering place for artists and creative thinkers from around the world, students of all ages and backgrounds, and audiences seeking extraordinary cultural enrichment.

LIBRARY OF CONGRESS CATALOGING-IN-PUBLICATION DATA
Names: Bierds, Linda, author.
Title: The Hardy tree / Linda Bierds.
Description: Port Townsend, Washington : Copper Canyon Press, [2019] |
Includes bibliographical references.
Identifiers: LCCN 2019018415 | ISBN 9781556595769 (softcover : acid-free paper)
Subjects: | GSAFD: Alternative histories (Fiction) | Biographical fiction.
Classification: LCC PS3552.I357 H37 2019 | DDC 813/.54—dc23
LC record available at https://lccn.loc.gov/2019018415

9 8 7 6 5 4 3 2 FIRST PRINTING

COPPER CANYON PRESS
Post Office Box 271
Port Townsend, Washington 98368
www.coppercanyonpress.org

FOR SYDNEY

CONTENTS

THE HARDY TREE

Self-Portrait: A Cento

I can't be alone in this,
the wars are everywhere, o even within.

Alone, I am nothing
and there's the shape of nothing caught in air:

an O without a figure,
grain of the night sky's empty hour.

I forget and remember and forget
the who I am and who are you, the who

too thin to cipher and with no start and end,
sewn together & torn again,

stretched out like variable stars,
like anyone's portrait as a path of ill-formed light.

PART ONE

Nabokov's Colored Hearing

I present a fine case of colored hearing. . . .
the color sensation seems to be produced
by the very act of my orally forming a given
letter while I imagine its outline.

Had my mother turned away from me
as I sat on the nursery floor, my alphabet blocks
leaning together in their unsteady towers,
had she laughed when I said their colors were wrong,
each raised wooden letter carved from some spectrum
I could not see, had my mother,
my fellow synesthete, not followed my eyes
as an *m* swelled in the air between us,
not listened as I said of its shape and sound,
"a fold of pink flannel," had my mother not seen,
as I did, *h* as a brown shoelace,
or the *z*'s thundercloud blue,
I would never have closed my eyes at night
to watch anything more on my inner lids
than a brush of retinal dust,
never have followed my curious alphabet
as its letters released their mysteries:
now walnuts rustling in a canvas sack,
now mirrors, harps, clouds of small parrots,
now box after box of humming hives,
and, just before sleep, pale keepers in veils
lifting the frames through the smoke.

Casabianca

italicized text by Alan Turing
(b. June 23, 1912–d. June 7, 1954)

Hazelhurst

Sussex

1923

Dear Mother and Daddy

*Guess what I am am writing with It is an invention of my own it is a fountain
pen like this:—*

A nib

B cork to stop ink and hold nib

C ink

D tube for ink

E squishy end of fountain pen/filler

F air

§ §

This was his path:
up Horsecastles Road
and Long Street,
left on St. Swithin's,
right on Newland,
left on the dogleg Avenue,
and into the garden
to count the bees,
to watch the shape
of their rise and dip,
their lateral flight
blossom to blossom to blossom.

§ §

Hazelhurst
Sussex

Dear Mother and Daddy

I was 2nd this week again. . . . There is a lecture tonmorow Wainwright was-
next to bottom this week

§ §

What is the pattern, insect to flower?
Where is the path, flower to hive?
How do vibration and message meet?
When does the body turn?

§ §

Hazelhurst
Sussex

Dear Mother and Daddy,

GB said that as I wrote so thick I was to get some new nibs from T. Wells and I
am writing with them now. this is my patent ink

§ §

Wilmslow Magistrates' Court
1952

The charge: Gross Indecency contrary to Section 11 of the Criminal Law
Amendment Act 1885

§ §

If the cells exist but cannot be found
If one crafts with invisible ink
If the pollen is thick
If the baskets fill unevenly
If one crafts with sound
If one crafts with flashing light
If the hive is a point on a lost line
If the body in motion slants

§ §

The Next Million Years
—Sir Charles Galton Darwin, 1952

. . . there might be a drug, which, without other harmful effects, removed
the urgency of sexual desire, and so reproduced in humanity the status of
workers in a beehive.

§ §

Hazelhurst
Sussex

Dear Mother and Daddy,

*I have got a lovely sort of cinema kind of thing You can draw new films for it.
There are sixteen pictures in each but I worked out that I could draw "The boy
stood at the tea table" you know the Rhyme made up from casabianca*

§ §

Wilmslow Magistrates' Court
1952

White male. Attitude: intransigent. Photographed. Fingerprinted.

§ §

The boy stood at the tea table
And saw within the grain
A lamp that lit both boy and whorls
And in the lamp a flame

That glowed then branched symmetrically
Across that mirrored world.
The patterns capturing the boy
Began within the whorls.

Ivory Tightrope Walker

Seventeenth century, use unknown

Not weather vane, not lightning rod,
although the slender figure, balanced
on a rooftop wire, might have drawn
what others called in time
ion strikes, their split and re-split light

branched downward like a willow.
Hip-high to a young child, geriatric,
eroded on his windward side,
he stood facing orchards and contoured fields,
while at his back, from surrounding seas,
his century's cargo sailed into the harbor.
Tulip bulbs. Heresy. Lenses to draw
the moon closer, lenses to enter a rice grain's starch.

Look to the sky for a sign and there he was,
afloat between roof tiles and a thundercloud's anvil.
Not folly. Not triumph. Not graven image.
Although whatever forces shaped him
began from instability, some atmospheric discontent
across the orchard, into the barn,
over the adze and fretsaw. Some restlessness

in the eye. Why else peel bark from pulp,
preen it in an acid bath, string a braided wire
along each stepless plantar arch?
Not completely understood—the impulse,
the form—even by the carver. Although

not without a glint of reason.
Look to the sky and there he was,
balanced, like the century, between

enigma and enlightenment. Sometimes
storms flashed toward him, cloud to ground,
and a rooftop spire kicked a return stroke
back to the sky. Sometimes the electrified earth
toppled whatever walked there. Over the clear air,
sometimes a sheet quivered, a long unfolding
across the blue. Silent, with no source at all.

Metamorphosis: 1680

> *I paint flowers decorated with caterpillars. . . .*
> *I want to inquire into everything that exists and*
> *find out how it began.*

Maria Sibylla Merian

> *From basil, the scorpion.*

Athanasius Kircher

From pine-tree resin, amber.
    From fury, hail.
From acacia's sap, the bond.
    From raindrops, frogs.
From clay, yellow ocher.
    From dust, fleas.
From the beetle, carmine.
    From mud, the beetle.
From the murex snail, violet.
    From sea-foam, the anchovy.
From the lamb, parchment.
    From the bull, the bee.
What?
    From the mouth of a slaughtered bull,
    cloaked in thyme and serpyllum,
    the bee.
From the sable, the brush tip.
    From books, the moth.
From the eagle, swan, crow, lark,
the diminishing quills.
    From fire, red snow, and the west wind,
    the worm.
From the worm, the silk moth.
    From vapor, the silk moth.

What? From the spun cocoon, the silk moth.

Yes. From steam and bluster,

the silk moth.

From the silk moth's mouth,

the potentate's cloak.

From the potentate's horse,

the hornet.

The Warboys Journal: One

Virginia Woolf at Seventeen

> *I must make some mark on paper. . . tho'*
> *my mark must be frail & somewhat disjointed.*

I am practicing my penmanship with various nibs, this one thin as the beak of a lark. Push, pull. Push, pull.

§ §

heroic resolution to change my ideas of calligraphy

dear but somewhat too romantic pen

This   This is written with my dear, but somewhat too

§ §

The village of Warboys rests in the Fens. On a padding of carpets I rest in our Punt, watching the wide sky, the lavish cloud conglomerations. High above me, tossed like embers, bats are catching the day's last light.

What a beautiful world we live in!

§ §

I am very sorry that I cannot find anyone
to agree in this matter with me.   This at last

This   This was one of the last things that

§ §

If I go on at this rate methinks I shall soon have finished this book—but the fever will not last—I know the disease well. The world, the word. On the road today to the Rectory: a horse cart, four windmills, pure air for fathoms & fathoms & acres & acres.

§ §

This I

This I write in the year of a

§ §

We traveled to Ramsey today, a market town on the border of the Fens. Running north, a wide street called the Great Whyte. When Oliver Cromwell's cousin longed for a new coat, fabric was sent to Ramsey from London. The year was 1666. Within the fabric's spun & twisted & polished threads, bubonic plague nested. The cousin, the tailor & 400 villagers died.

§ §

This sheet of paper if it had followed the fate

Within the fabric's polished

§ §

Clouds today & mist, but as we drove along, the sun shot a shaft of light down & we beheld a glorious expanse of sky & far away over the flat fields a spire caught the beam & glittered like a gem in the darkness & wetness of the surrounding countries.

§ §

Usages of linen predate the book & still

fabric   spindle   spire   beam

the glory grows & still we

§ §

How can things so finely made unmake us so completely?

Self-Portrait, 2016: A Fusion

Tonight & last night we began our Sugar campaign. . .
the most scientific way of catching moths.

Virginia Woolf

The mysteries of mimicry had a special attraction
for me.

Vladimir Nabokov

When they grew too thick,
the gradually darkening days,
when the months were too thick
and the olive and pink hummingbird moths
sank through the sparse lilacs—I was a child,
I could hear them thwirring—
everything shifted. Not in an instant,
but steadily, as a specimen shifts
in a swab of ether.
          Frost, nightfall—
that steadier diminishment.
I sugared the tree trunks with rum and molasses.
And although, each evening,
the cycle was always the same—
enchantment, deception, enchantment—still,
I would hold my face close to the bark
when my lantern first flared
and whatever moth was sipping the syrup
drew back its gray primaries
and flashed toward my partially lighted shape
two crimson underwing irises,
one hundred, no, five hundred times greater
than the moth's own eyes.

Always the same—
I was a child, enchantment's prey,
deception's prey—how the eyes
had no corresponding body,
and the gray primaries lifted and fell,
lifted and fell, until the seen shape
and the shape I could not unsee
rose together to tap on my lantern.

Silk Hall: Sherborne School, 1929

I want to say how sorry I am about Chris. . .

Of course I simply worshipped the ground he trod on—
a thing which I did not make much attempt to disguise,
I am sorry to say.

Alan Turing

Imagine three boys: A, C, and E.
Of the three, one—Edward VI—is made of stained glass.
He sits on a stained-glass throne
in the library window of this ancient school.
From a small table, A and I—I am C—are watching him,
or better, watching the glass flare and darken
as the afternoon's clouds interrupt the sun.

The figure we make, A to C to E to A,
has no equal sides or angles, like a sail,
or the stars in Libra's balance beam.
Or the jagged path desire takes, A for me—
I have known this always—Edward and I
for the clean, unobstructed pillow of air
three stained-glass angels anchor.

Given two points, Euclid wrote,
there is one straight line that joins them.
And the line uniting Edward to me
is a rod-shaped bacillus already thriving
in our young lungs.

Still, today is pleasant and E is breathing effortlessly,
light, then shadow, ruffling his ermine lapels.

This room was once a silk mill. And there,
between A and the fourth set of open bookshelves,
books of silk were cut into *mosses,*
mosses cut into *slips.* Think of the din,
A says—too loudly—the reeling and twisting,
the clack of the tiered frames.

I think instead of the sorting: coarse from fine.
The frayed and dissimilar, the nibby and doubtful removed.

A gave to me once a star globe—glass orb of a lampshade
filled with plaster—his inked-in constellations
so finely done I could trace the Winter Triangle,
could imagine how, from one corner,
rays from Orion's hand
reached out equally, both for the dog
and the mystery that comes before the dog.

I fear for A, loud and gritty and brilliant.
Although A fears nothing,
cupped as he is—so securely—
between thought and phenomena.

The rod-shaped bacilli I carry
advance in waxy capsules, invisible to the unaided eye.
The silk-making larva
swings its entirely visible head, back and forth,
back and forth, three hundred thousand times,
weaving its tight cocoon. A says
that the looping motion, over and under and over again,
traces the sign for infinity. Unendingness.
For the silk, perhaps. But not

for the never-to-be moth, popped in its woven case
with the slimmest of silver pins.
But carefully popped, A says, so as not to pierce
the pattern, which could in an ideal world
stretch for a mile in a single line.

And often I think of that line,
weightless, almost transparent, running, like history,
from the ancient crucible over Edward's head
down toward our wide shoreline,
where men in black boots, under a circle
of screaming gulls, wrench
everything history's tide has uncovered
up from the sucking mud.

On the Somme

italicized line by Wilfred Owen

Listen. Is that the enemy   rustling just beyond the wires?
Or rabbits, ground birds,   a little mud-filled wind, warm
on the blasted meadow?   My mother could play, between
her upright thumbs,   a different note from every spike
or blade of meadow grass   she picked. Sweet hays, vernals,
the greens, blue-greens,   the almost-blacks. Cup your hands
to form a cave, she said—   Why have I remembered this?—
place your lips against   the blade—Is memory the
enemy?—and blow across   the gap. My thumbs were small.
The sounds I made were   shrill as Škoda shells,
no matter the source,   no matter how my breathing shifted.
Back to the field   the spent reeds dropped, and whatever
birds I had silenced   sang again from the hedgerows.
Cup your hands   to form a simple room.
Listen. Is that the—   My breath, first cool,
then warm, fills   my palms like smoke.
No sound, but deep   within the vacancy
I see a hearth,   a parlor's sheen,
some listening shape,   eternal near a window.
And each slow dusk   a drawing-down of blinds.

Wartime Domicilium: A Cento

lines by Thomas Hardy, Vladimir Nabokov, and
Rupert Brooke

It faces west, and round the back and sides
High beeches, bending, hang a veil of boughs.
Here was my bedroom, now reserved for guests,
Shapeless and slow, unsteady and opaque.
Here is the ancient floor,
And a loosened slate,
By the false azure in the windowpane.

And there's the wall of sound: the nightly wall,
Behind the gateways of the brain.
On the balcony
And a pond edged with grayish leaves,
Such arrows of rain!

I heard the pale skies fall apart,
Felt the quick stir of wonder, sat alone.

What is it, in the self's eclipse,
When the white flame in us is gone
And form and line and solid follow?

Here was the former door,
And we have come into our heritage:

From left to right the blank page of the road,
The fiery windows, and the stream
Of wretched memorial stones—

Mysterious, and shape to shape,
Like chastened children sitting silent in a school.
Down their carved names the raindrop ploughs.

The Bird Trap

after the painting by Pieter Brueghel the Younger

But for clusters of red clothing, the painting
is monochrome, snow and river
in that ivory-going-to-gray a winter evening offers.

And under the evening, under
the sky and smoky horizon, traversing
the painting's lower half, deep snow and the frozen river
exactly divide the scene:

two dozen birds near a riverfront yard, six of them flying;
two dozen people on the ice, six with arms extended.

And under their laughter and guttural chirrups
lies nothing but the scrape of skates
and the dull chatter of curling stones
as they slip, like great rounds of granite bread,
toward some gradually vanishing target
etched on the scored ice.

§ §

Movements Alan Turing would love, had he seen the painting.
The balancing figures, of course, and the curler,
bent to a stone, putting a little English on it.
But also the target, invisibly sinking away—
rings, inner rings, and a center button—becoming
at last just a pattern in the mind.

§ §

It is 1952. The charge: gross indecency. The parlor:
cluttered. On a cheap violin, Turing is playing
"Cockles and Mussels," the music's wordless barrow
scraping past Wills and Rimmer, two seated detectives
who cannot stop mouthing sweet Molly Malone. Why not,
for these minutes, listen, the bugger so welcoming,
so quick to confess, as if two men together. . . as if
two men complicitly trying
the three condemned exchanges Turing so openly listed,
were free? And isn't it almost legal, he asked,
and who is displaced, the world so shattered
we must speak in codes, in key-clicks and ciphers,
rings, inner rings, the bow lifted, his unshaven chin
on the rest, breath in, breath out, fogging
the body, fogging the thin, yellowed,
almost mother-of-pearl varnish, over
and over, alive, alive-o.

§ §

Two perils: in the lower-left foreground
a large, dark hole in the ice; in the lower right
a bird trap—a heavy, wooden door
propped up at one end by a stick.

It makes a little lean-to, a little respite
in the snow, its soft floor sprinkled with seeds,

and its trip rope, tied to the stick, so pale
in the winter yard that Turing must step closer,
must place his face near the old wood
and stiffened leather hinges

to see the rope arc upward—from the stick, through
the yard, then on through a narrow window
where someone invisibly watches.

Or doesn't. The window so close to the painting's edge
the trap seems harmless, unmanned, a simple
geometric shape, a kind of static pendulum
set to capture the turning world. And did they know,

§ §

Turing asked, that the proper way
to launch a pendulum's bob
is by thread and candle flame? The bob
tied above its downward arc, the candle
burning through the tie. Foucault—more wine?—
knew this. Did they? No chance for interference then.
No clammy hands or coughs or tics.
No common human veerings.

§ §

The house is almost outside the scene. A slice
of wall and roofline, a slash of bird-blind window.

In the foreground, left and right,
two perils, passive: allegory's lolling greed.

§ §

One takes the utmost care, he said.
Clear path. Near-windless room. Star shape
painted on the floor to illustrate the journey.

Symmetry. Trajectory.

Bright candle. Silk thread.

PART TWO

Bone Cockerel: Norman Cross Prisoner-of-War Camp, England

circa 1800, bones on wooden armature. Carver
unknown.

Any year, in any tilting hemisphere,
any set of bones, split and polished, gathered
from the cooking pots. . . But I am—
this hour—here, he wrote, my art a single shape lifted
from whatever squealed or snarled or lowed across
war's holding pen. Just touch and feathered bones hatched
into a bird, a set of wings, a textured silence throughout
a cape and blade, a blackened eye that looked
at soot and grain and linseed oil. I,
the prisoner wrote, I am here. My days are aimed
as light is aimed, shaft by shaft across a turning armature.

§ §

As light is aimed, shaft by shaft across a turning armature,
the prisoner wrote, I am here. My days are aimed
at soot and grain and linseed oil. I:
a cape and blade, a blackened eye that looked
into a bird, a set of wings, a textured silence throughout
war's holding pen. Just touch and feathered bones hatched
from whatever squealed or snarled or lowed across
this hour. Here, he wrote: my art, a single shape lifted
from the cooking pots. . . But I am
any set of bones, split and polished, gathered
any year, in any tilting hemisphere.

Identity Matrix: Alan Turing, 1952

one	said	mathematics	is	the	music	of	reason
and	one	said	the	bunting	in	spring	withdraws
increasingly	the	one	singing	in	chorus	isolates	itself
nothing	music	made	one	winter	lifts	off	immeasurably
figurations	of	value	said	one	can	nest	empty-setted
that	buntings	withdraw	increasingly	said	one	is	paradox
measure	is	every	silence	canceled	gather	one	dividing
diminishment	loss	vacancy	then	soundlessness	nothing	following	one

Lessons of the War: Deviant Identity Formations

italicized lines by Henry Reed

You must never be over-sure. You must say, when reporting:
  I am a girl, but without the proper balance?
Well that, for an answer, is what we rightly call—
  Evasive? Disguised?—
Moderately satisfactory only, the reason being—
  I am in the wrong body but with the right mind?—
Is that two things have been omitted, and those are very important.
  That my safety catch is always released?
That things only seem to be things.
  Yes, I know, and that what will defeat me
Glistens like coral in all of the neighboring gardens.

This is the lower sling swivel. And this—
  Looks like our swing set's swivel—
Is the upper sling swivel, whose use you will see.
  I remember its sound, just under the crossbar!
I am sure that's quite clear; and suppose, for the sake of example—
  That a sling swings my body in every direction—
There may be dead ground in between.
  Between each of my upward arcs? My unbalanced feet?
The ever-important question of human balance—
  Rests on our sling swivels, doesn't it? Which only seem to be things—

Is one which need not delay us. Again, you know—
  The basics: That a breech is nothing if not open—
That maps are of time, not place, so far as the army—
  That what will defeat me grows by accretion, like coral—
Happens to be concerned—the reason being—
  That being is all—

Is very important. Perhaps you may never get—

That almond branches, like the solitary, hold silent but eloquent gestures—

The knack of judging a distance, but at least you know—

That you showed me the branches, and the bees fumbling the flowers—

The various holds and rolls and throws and breakfalls

With which place, not time, will assault me.

And the various holds and rolls and throws and breakfalls—

Depend on human balance?—

Which in our case we have not got—

Go on. The various holds and rolls. . .

Lie gently together. Which is, perhaps, only to say—

The landscape is motionless?—

Perhaps I was never in a strong position—

And the branches reach out without reaching?—

Or the ball of my foot got hurt, or I had some weakness—

With your proper issue?—

Which you may sometimes meet.

I have met fear, and a bit of joy, its bolts easing the spring.

And how far away, would you say? And do not forget—

How far away the fear? The joy?—

How to report on a landscape: the central sector.

A boot-sole away, from dead ground to the ball of my foot.

I have been here before. But somehow then—

The central sector encircles us, doesn't it?—

I was the tied-up one. How to get out—

Be ready and not over-sure?

The readiness is all. How can I help but feel—

And the being. The being and the readiness are all—

Silent in all of the gardens and the bees going backwards and forwards—

And the fears and the bolts and

The human beings now: in what direction are they?

Secure Speech Cipher System

Bell Laboratories, 1943

To be nothing but the sound of hornets,
that was the goal for the human voice, Ally to Ally,
each wind-filled, greening word whittled to a thread.
The cipherists filled one top-secret cell, near-nothingness

their goal, the human voice encoded, Ally to Ally.
De-pulse the pitch, de-tone the wave, de-spec the spectrum—
the cipherists filled one top-secret cell with nothing more
than filaments of numerals. Then built them back, re-toned

the pulse, re-pitched the wave, re-speckled the spectrum,
as one might—instantly—rebuild a leopard from a paw print.
From filaments of numerals they built a voice, and from
the voice a prophecy—nicknamed X, for what was almost there.

Daily from its paw print, the leopard instantly stepped,
while from adjacent cells, deciphered Axis codes bloomed,
nicknamed not for X but for a there that always was.
The SS code was *quince.* Rommel's words were *chaffinch.*

Up from Axis codes, deciphered cells bloomed, or flew,
or swam, as if the natural world might mend the broken word.
The SS code was *quince.* Then *chaffinch, limpet,*
seahorse, sunfish, trumpeter, pike,

as if the natural world might mend the broken word.
Near last to fall was *plaice,* which to the ear, just after
seahorse, sunfish, trumpeter, pike,
inexactly doubles back—both creature and its habitat.

Near last to fall was place, just after "old procedures"—
masquerades and vinegar ink, trench-coated agents
who inexactly doubled back, creatures to their habitats.
This was the world's new war, the war's new

prophecy: past masquerades and vinegar ink,
a wind-filled, greening world whittled to a thread.
This was the war's new word, the word's new war—
there and there, nothing but the sound of hornets.

The Underwings of War

National Pigeon Service, England, 1940

Notch.
Web.
And then,
down the shaft,
lesser wing-coverts
and marginal coverts, and soft,
greater underwing coverts—although never as great
as greater under-primary
coverts, gray-coated
and down-plumped,
trailing
what
might
reveal
a pattern
just over the down
that might support a secrecy.
Launched from double-decker buses, or attic windows,
or the dark roofs at Bletchley Park,
the lesser pigeons,
always first
to find
the
fray,
sport black
metallic
canisters strapped to
matted lapel feathers. And tucked
inside, like Russian dolls, a cipher's hollow chambers—

down and down, a Fibonacci

spiral, a paper

nautilus

of words

and

codes

and keys

that shift with

each decipherment.

The bard is in the wand—read space

as shape, read *a* as *i*—the key takes subterfuge,

that doubling, double agency

when tomfoolery

is crossed with

rage. But

these

are

simply

carriers,

word-burdened, instinct-

tossed, searching for the perch within

a blasted atmosphere. Find forms, the message says, and

everything will fall in line.

The bird is in the

wind. The loft

is in

the

smoke.

Encryption

Near Dorset's western coast, its beaches
brittle with ammonite husks and the *tip, tap, tip*
of hammers and fossil picks, near white cliffs
and a black river, up through meadows and down
through nineteen layers of quarried limestone,
the idea for a code begins.
From the quarrymen's bed names,
from the pressures of war or entombment or song,
an untraceable shape steps, layer
by limestone layer, straight from Pig's Dirt
to Lower Verity, the span of those first strata
just what encryption requires: one sow, one position,
and the clickety-click of truth and dirt.
Then it climbs, the code, past
Lower Skulls, Under Copper, Upper Skulls,
and just beneath Mongrel, Specketty.
Specketty. Nothing but sound, saw-toothed,
off-throwing. That is the key, isn't it?
Follow the bed names, the patternless patterns:
fact, sound, position, illusion. *Tip. Tap.*
Top Copper, Top Tape, Third Quick, Rattle.
Then turn from the clicking, climb back
through form, Grey Ledge, three Fish Beds—soft,
off-throwing—and just at the last,
on either side of Upper Verity:
Glass Bottle and the Unnamed Doggers.
That is the path, isn't it? That secrecy takes?
Begin with a beast in its sty.
End with an unnamed sense of pursuit
and a fixed, unbreakable shape,
age-stained just a step beyond clarity.

Evolution

How, Alan Turing thought, does the soft-walled,
jellied, symmetrical cell
become the asymmetrical horse? It was just before dusk,
the sun's last shafts doubling the fence posts,
all the dark mares on their dark shadows. It was just
after Schrödinger's *What is Life?*
not long before Watson, Franklin, Crick, not long before
supper. How does a chemical soup,
he asked, give rise to a biological pattern? And how
does a pattern shift, an outer ear
gradually slough its fur, or a shorebird's stubby beak
sharpen toward the trout?
He was halfway between the war's last enigmas
and the cyanide apple—two bites—
that would kill him. Halfway along the taut wires
that hummed between crime
and pardon, indecency and privacy. How do solutions,
chemical, personal, stable, unstable,
harden into shapes? And how do shapes break?
What slips a microfissure
across a lightless cell, until time and matter
double their easy bickering? God?
Chance? A chemical shudder? He was happy and not,
tired and not, humming a bit
with the fence wires. How does a germ split to a self?
And what is a—*We are not our acts
and remembrances,* Schrödinger wrote. *Should something—*
God, chance, a chemical shudder?—
sever us from all we have been, still it would not kill us.
It was just before dusk, his segment
of earth slowly ticking toward night. Like time, he thought,
we are almost erased by rotation,

as the dark, symmetrical planet lifts its asymmetrical cargo
up to the sunset: horses, ryegrass—
In no case, then, is there a loss of personal existence to deplore—
marten, whitethroat, blackbird,
lark—*nor will there ever be.*

Lunar Eclipse

Mount Rainier National Park

We are standing on the access road to Paradise.
Seven miles from the gates. *We are standing*
on the centerline, the moon on our faces, the mountain
at our backs. Were it less than full, we might see,
in its northwest sector, the Land of Snow
and the Ocean of Storms. *Because it is full, we can see,*
just over our shoulders, how the Ramparts climb up
toward the glaciers. We might see, near the Sea
of Showers, the dark-floored crater of Plato.
How the glaciers, just over our shoulders—
Pyramid, Kautz, Nisqually—shine. How the spreading
bedrock shines. As if we are starting again,
we have placed—there—on the moon's widening shadow
Kepler, Copernicus, Archimedes, Aristoteles.
And opened a Sea of Fertility. A Sea of Nectar.
As if we imagine   *a harvest.*
No sound it seems, on the slopes, in the firs.
Nothing hoots. Nothing calves. *Although*
through Nisqually's steep moraine, rocks
must be shifting, grasses cinching their eternal grip.
Look, in the blackness, how the moon's rim glows,
like a ring from an ancient astrolabe.
We are standing in the roadway. There is nothing
on our faces but the glow of refracted dust.
At our backs, the mountain is shifting, aligning itself
with the passing hours. First ice. Then stone.
Then the ice-green grasses. *We are standing*
on the centerline   aligning ourselves with the earth.
We are standing on the access road   as if we imagine

an eternal grip. *Look—they are rotating on, now.*
Already a pale crescent spreads
past the Known Sea   *and the Muir Snowfield—*
as if we are starting. . . *—past*
the Trail of the Shadows, the ice-green grasses,
the seas of nectar, the craters of rest,
the gardens of   nothing but passing hours.

Pulse

On the pulse
the bee
and on the bee
the hive
and on the hive
the autumn snow
that pulse and bee
have warmed into
a moon-shaped dip
and on the dip
a vacancy
and on the moon
eclipse

PART THREE

Magna Carta: An Embroidery

On June 15, 2015, the 800th anniversary of Magna Carta, London's British Library displayed *Magna Carta (An Embroidery),* a nearly thirteen-meter-long tapestry imagined by artist Cornelia Parker and stitched by Parker and 201 others. In minute detail the embroidery reproduces the entire Wikipedia article on Magna Carta as it appeared on June 15, 2014. All that a visitor to the page would have seen is stitched there: Wikipedia's logo, search box, and sidebar, and the Charter's seemingly endless refinements, as a land and its people were embellished by words and annulments. The article's few illustrations, including likenesses of Pope Innocent III and Edward Coke, are precisely rendered. Words printed in blue are stitched in blue: Castle, River Thames, fish weirs, supremacy, Random article, Offences Against the Person Act. Even the scarlet flushes on Innocent's cheeks, like tiny suns near the sides of his nose, mirror the page's image. "It's a hand-wrought thing," Parker said. Like the Wikipedia article, the tapestry and the Charter itself are multiauthored, hand-wrought things.

Most of the text was embroidered by prisoners trained in creative needlework. Other stitchers included lawyers and judges; filmmakers and clerics; barons, baronesses, librarians, musicians, psychoanalysts, activists, students, and children. Together they traced Magna Carta's evolution as, gradually sloughing its clauses away, it moved past the feudal barons it protected—and the serfs it ignored—to enter modern statute. Of the few words remaining on the books today, these are the most directly referenced:

"No free man shall be seized or imprisoned, or stripped of his rights or possessions, or outlawed or exiled, or deprived of his standing in any other way, nor will we proceed with force against him, or send others to do so, except by the lawful judgment of his equals or by the law of the land. To no one will we sell, to no one deny or delay right of justice."

As special as the parchment they were written on, these phrases, and Magna Carta's sentences in general, nevertheless impacted very few lives. Their domain was the free man, not the unfree peasantry, which constituted the majority of the population. Neither was the Charter concerned with trial by jury or habeas corpus; these issues would be covered over time. "Its authority and influence," wrote Shami Chakrabarti, of Britain's National Council for Civil Liberties, "may derive more from what people think it said, rather than that which was actually penned; but the unreal can be more powerful than the real; and so it proved with Magna Carta."

§ §

To begin the project, Parker transferred Wikipedia's article as a printed pattern to a long swath of cotton fabric, then cut the fabric into eighty-seven sections to be circulated among the embroiderers. To end the project, she placed long mirrors under the tapestry so that viewers could see "the backstory," "the history of the work," could see the way phrases cross the cotton like bird tracks, unpatterned, just under the promise and confines of words; the way "oath" and "King," and "law" and "land," and "water" and "meadow" seem almost to touch.

Seen from below, "held without charge," stitched by Moazzam Begg after his detainment at Guantánamo Bay, is as fractured as history; so too are the tightly bound words of baronesses: "justice," "denial," "delay." One embroidered illustration near the tapestry's end, of a small memorial to Magna Carta, is as clear from below as it is from above, each of the structure's pale columns equally straight against a forested background. Only the tree limbs blow in reverse, top view and bottom, and the few small clouds enter the scene from opposite directions.

It's a quiet setting, not far from the water-meadow where King John sealed Magna Carta. He was quiet himself that day, knowing the gesture was empty, knowing the first of the charter's multiple annulments was already fluttering toward him from the papacy. Erasure. . . annulment. . . refinement . . . annulment. . . erasure—so it would be then, for years and years to come, five linked shapes that advanced through the grasses continuously.

What began from the need to restrict one man's power seems not to have ended easily.

It isn't clear which prisoner refused to embroider into his assigned phrase the words "habeas corpus," but a judge filled them in for him. And the name of the embroiderer whose "freedoms that supposedly existed" was stitched so perfectly isn't available easily. Nor does the tapestry's guidebook tell us how long the journey would have taken from the meadow to the castle, or how lasting the seal's wax. But it does point out that, in the article's section on Edward Coke, just above the phrase "Petition of Right," the word "liberty" was stitched by Edward Snowden.

Magna Carta: An Erosion

On June 15, 2015, the 800th anniversary of Magna Carta, London's British Library displayed *Magna Carta (An Embroidery)*, a nearly thirteen-meter-long tapestry **imagine**d by artist Cornelia Parker **and** stitched by Parker and 201 others. In minute detail the **embroidery** reproduces the entire Wikipedia article on Magna Carta as it appeared on June 15, 2014. All that a visitor to the page would have seen is stitched there: Wikipedia's logo, search box, and sidebar, and the Charter's seemingly endless refinements, as **a land and its people** were **embellished by words and** annulments. The **a**rticle's **few illustrations** including likenesses of Pope Innocent III and Edward Coke, are precisely rendered. Words printed in blue are stitched in blue: Castle, **River** Thames, **fish weirs,** supremacy, **Random** article, Offences Against the **Person** Act. Even the scarlet flushes on Innocent's cheeks, **like tiny suns near the sides of his** nose, mirror the page's **image.** "It's a hand-wrought thing," Parker said. Like the Wikipedia article, the tapestry and the Charter itself are multiauthored, hand-wrought things.

   Most of the text was embroidered by prisoners trained in creative needlework. Other stitchers included lawyers and judges; filmmakers and clerics; barons, baronesses, librarians, musicians, psychoanalysts, activ**is**ts, students, and children. Together they traced Magna Carta's evolution as, **gradually sloughing** its clauses **away**, it moved past the feudal barons it protected—and the serfs it ignored—to enter modern statute. **Of the few words remaining** on the books today, **these are the most dire**ctly referenced:

   "No free man shall be seized or imprisoned, or stripped of **his rights** or possessions, or outlawed or exiled, or deprived of his standing in any other way, nor **will** we **proceed with force against him,** or send others to do so, except by the lawful judgment of his equals or by the law of the land. To no one will we sell, to no one deny or delay right of justice."

   As special **as** the **parchment** they were written on, these phrases, and Magna Carta's **sentences** in general, never**the**less impacted very few **lives.** Their domain was the free man, not the unfree peasantry, which constituted the majority of the population. Ne**it**her was the Charter concerned with trial by jury or habeas corpus; these issues would be **covered** over time. "Its authority and influence," wrote Shami Chakrabarti, of Britain's National Council for Civil Liberties, "may derive more from what people think it said, rather than that which was actually penned; but the unreal can be more powerful than the real; and so it proved with Magna Carta."

§ §

To begin the project, Parker transferred Wikipedia's article as a printed pattern to a long swath of cotton fabric, then cut the fabric into eighty-seven sections to be circulated among the embroiderers. To end the project, she placed long mirrors under the tapestry so that viewers could see "the backstory," "the history of the work," could see the way phrases cross the cotton like bird tracks, unpatterned, just under the promise and confines of words; the way "oath" and "King," and "law" and "land," and "water" and "meadow" seem almost to touch.

Seen from below, "held without charge," stitched by Moazzam Begg after his detainment at Guantánamo Bay, is as fractured as history; so too are the tightly bound words of baronesses: "justice," "denial," "delay." One embroidered illustration near the tapestry's end, of a small memorial to Magna Carta, is as clear from below as it is from above, each of the structure's pale columns equally straight against a forested background. Only the tree limbs blow in reverse, top view and bottom, and the few small clouds enter the scene from opposite directions.

It's a quiet setting, not far from the water-meadow where King John sealed Magna Carta. He was quiet himself that day, knowing the gesture was empty, knowing the first of the charter's multiple annulments was already fluttering toward him from the papacy. Erasure. . . annulment. . . refinement . . . annulment. . . erasure—so it would be then, for years and years to come, five linked shapes that advanced through the grasses continuously.

What began from the need to restrict one man's power seems not to have ended easily.

It isn't clear which prisoner refused to embroider into his assigned phrase the words "habeas corpus," but a judge filled them in for him. And the name of the embroiderer whose "freedoms that supposedly existed" was stitched so perfectly isn't available easily. Nor does the tapestry's guidebook tell us **how long the journey** would have taken from the meadow to the castle, or **how lasting** the seal's wax. But it does point out that, in the **a**rticle's section on Edward Coke, just above the phrase "Petition of Right," the word "**liberty**" was **stitched by** Edward **Snow**den.

PART FOUR

Color: An Elegy

The yellow reflected by the bee's thorax
and scientist's sleeve, by the gold-topped glint
of seven entomology pins, no longer exists,
its formula—lead-tin, fire, the binder's precise
environment—lost.
                        And the mineral green
of the shallow spoon at the bee's tongue-tip exists
but is gone: too much heat or chill or the complex
erosions of light.
                        Almost gone but fully there,
the semitransparent, outstretched wing
is as finely leaded as the room's distant window,
painted in shaky perspective
but offering, with the wing, a brushstroke
of philosophical symmetry: how thin the membranes
that free us from the world.
                        Although the world
of 1637, its gradually rising, tinted ground,
has climbed through the huge, anatomical bee,
the hind legs and faded pollen basket,
has climbed through the pins
and window, which is, in fact,
                        outside the frame
but bright on the curve of the bee's black eye.
There, and also there, the silk-sleeved figure
of Song Yingxing once bent in reflection
across the panes. That is our earth, he said,
stopped in the prism
                        of an insect's eye:
catties of copper, wagons of loam, bronze hives
like lamps on the cliffsides. And the five

enduring grains, the greens, the reds,
the ungreenable whites—

                                This is beauty's way,
isn't it? Song once said: On the finite curve
of a bee's dark eye, all that light can carry
across a harrowed land.

Camouflage

A dressing up or painting out.
A spray of shoots across a mottled stratagem.

This was the task: with paint and wood and steel
replicate a willow, the one in any no-man's-land,

thick-trunked and pollarded. And turn,
in turn, the replica into an eight-foot periscope

where anyone might sit and watch an enemy
slip across a blasted field like murky water.

Or watch the cloud gas billow closer.
(It smelled like hay. So many poisons

smell like hay. Or lilacs. Or geraniums.)
The task? To craft a tree for camouflage

that anyone might climb, and crouch within,
and wait to hear the handbells ring All Clear—

a momentary, clappered joy, some said, up
from the horizontal belfries of the trenches.

And then the masks came off.
When Alan Turing died from cyanide,

he smelled like burnt almonds. Every organ,
the coroner said, smelled like burnt almonds.

Some need resemblances that tie us to the earth,
a metaphoric dressing up or painting out.

Lilacs, almonds, geraniums, hay. Willow, willow.
Some need the opposite.

Some said the bells were birds—salvation larks.

Some said he simply smelled like smoke.

Zeppelins

On nights when darkness was almost complete,
Zeppelins followed the glow of the Thames
to locate London. Like a sudden moon, the fleeing said,
when searchlights clicked on and a massive, white,
gondola-cratered fullness loomed overhead.
A moon, except for the shape, elongate, not round.
Except for the terrible drumming. More like a city,
they said, its girders and steel wires, its terrible

drumming. A city and a countryside, the hydrogen bladders
made from cotton and the guts of a nation's cows.
Or more like a crossing of earth and moon, eclipsed
by fire when incendiary bullets caught it.
Although most simply climbed away—membrane, pilots,
city, field—drumming nations lighter than air.

The Christmas Truce: 1914

It seems as if a storm glass holds us he said
its curious barometer

Late day and frost
thick on the mud and shattered trees
the sod that capped the periscopes

I would watch
the shapes the crystals made

And then the hymns began

rising in silence up through the glass

from opposite trenches
Stille Nacht   The First Noel

before rain
something like a moon

The war was young

before wind
something like a leaf

We had not met
the gasses yet

I would watch the shapes
the solution made

And when we walked
toward no-man's-land our boots
kicked up a shapelessness

if fixed
undisturbed   not exposed to
radiation

Merry Christmas Englishmen

a moon
rising in silence up from the base

Take your captives

and a bit of tobacco

a moon   a leaf   the splayed ribs

of a tree

Tomorrow is another day

Marking the Swans: Stanley Spencer at War

after the painting *Swan Upping at Cookham, 1915–1919*

From my north-aisle pew, I could hear
the river's boatmen
and the swans hissing, the pens and cobs
hissing, beating the water
with their wide wings. All up! the boatmen called,
herding the birds
toward the grassy bank. I could hear the words
move toward me, down
through the centuries, down through the unions
of beauty and greed,
as the cygnets chirped, feet scarred for the ancient Wardens,
beaks nicked for the ancient Guilds—
All up!—I rose—pale, tepid legs banded
for the Worshipful Company
of Dyers, or the King, or the Keeper of Suns—
All up!—and I rose with the swans
through the green bank of the chancel's light, unharmed
in that hour as they would be,
the most weightless of collars awaiting me.

§ §

Could you send me another sketchbook?
I draw nothing it seems but patients.

This morning, sunlight was blazing
down the hospital corridor, just near
the Sergeant-Major and his dog, and the men
were quiet, talking of crops and kit bags.
I was scrubbing the floor. Back and forth,

back and forth—abrasion, relief—
until the grain rose and light inched past
the sleeping dog to shine on the first cots.

I longed to paint the peace I felt
and then on the cots
the lobed heart of war fluttered
and a great clammy death began.
The day did not seem like day to me
and the men did not belong to day.

§ §

The Worshipful Company of Vintners
once marked swan beaks with the shape
of a spearhead. And on either side,
two dots like eyes. As the cygnet grew
did the spearhead lengthen and the eyes widen?

My painting is propped on my bedroom wall
hundreds of miles away. We both seem less
than half-finished: a few clouds in our upper quadrant,
and a deep, pale emptiness below.

§ §

Thank you for the pencils and St. Augustine's words.
All is not holy, I know, but I find that state
in whatever I draw now: gate posts
and lockers and water-bottles.
The horse-drawn travois. The sheets
on the wounded men.

§ §

Often, years ago, when the day
was too dark for painting, I stood on a little landing

to look toward an over-grown yew hedge
and the spindle-like trees rising above it.
Into the branches a black-bird would come, making
a circle of darkness on the fading sky.
Around me—have I told you this?—
the odors of oil lifted from the canvas
and the black-bird called and called from its branches
until suddenly it dropped diagonally
to sleep in a deeper darkness. I waited each time
for owls to start in the chestnuts, marking
the silence, loving that liminal place
between black-bird and owl, evening and night.
Art's timeless space. It grows harder

to use that word. Three high ravines stood out
from the snow today like three spear wounds.

§ §

Thank you for the paints and biscuits.
I am back from the outpost, back
from the shrapnel and sniping, the sense
of someone always just out of view.

From the dug-out where I crouched, I never saw
the enemy, but felt him pass just yards away
and heard the gravel crunch under his wagon wheels.
I never entered no-man's land by any light
brighter than the palest moon, never clearly saw
the shapes that filled me with their scents,
the wash of flowers all down Macedonia's low ravines,
the wash of ferns and flowers along the wire
we patrolled. And the almost-seen that filled me
in the almost-light: the fearful,
wondrous mystery: the enemy.

§ §

I dreamed of a swan, wings roped
to its white body. A swan and a boatman
and an emptiness. And now I am home,
the dream solid on the canvas before me
and the war a dream. Was I there those years?
The question is gone in an instant.
There is yellow lyddite on my fingers—
or whatever the enemy used in their shells.
A hint of explosive powder tracing my nails.
Barium. Cadmium. Ochre. Chrome.
I will wash it away at the well.

Lepidopteran: A Cento

lines and phrases by Vladimir Nabokov, Alan Turing,
and Thomas Hardy

In. . . the whitish muslin of a wide-mouthed net,
in time of the breaking of nations,
and in elementary arithmetic,

the lichen-gray primaries
keep in sufficiently close touch
as to impose one part of the pattern onto another.

The vibrational halo
of the string figures
passing from flower to flower,

border to border—
night-moths of measureless size,
circling

among the young, among the weak and old,
hawk moths at dusk
hatching

the war-adept in the mornings—
the vibrational halo
near the great wings

is not the judgment-hour,
only thin smoke without flame
written on terrestrial things.

I confess I do not believe in time.
And the highest enjoyment of timelessness
is an imitation game. . . filled with

the mysteries of mimicry. . . . But
when a certain moth resembles a certain wasp
and a deadly cipher

flaps its glad green leaves like wings,
what is our solution?
Peace on earth and silence in the sky?

I think that is not
the faith and fire within us. . . . Still,
I look into the depth of

each breeding-cage,
each floating-point form
cleft into light and shade,

hoping it might be so.

The Hive at Kew Gardens, 2016

*At present I am. . . working on. . . my mathematical
theory of embryology. . . symmetrical structures. . .
flowers. . . leaf arrangement. . .*

Alan Turing, 1951

From a distance, it seems
the thinnest of funnel clouds, or—yes—
all the land's bees swarming.
But this is the art of science, and we are inside it—
a forty-ton honeycomb of air and aluminum wire.
A latticed sculpture, seventeen meters high.
Bend closer, someone says—we can almost see,
in the meadow below us, the tiny, living hive
that sets these wires humming.
And now we are holding between our lips
flat, almost weightless, wooden sticks
that, touched to the lattice, transfer the bees' language
through the bones of our heads: the piping and begging,
the tooting and quacking. . . And how is it done,

this invisible relay, bee to vibration to us?
You would have loved the circuitry, those smallest
of sounds, tucked deep in a flowering hedge,
swelling upward and outward
to fill a hiveful of stick-biting minds.
And far below us, the inflorescence you tracked,
stem to stem, the leaves, one, one, two, three,
the codes that set the shapes, the clicks that set
them ticking. There and there,
the marigolds lift their flattened crowns
like trays of the smallest flowers.
Capitula. Bend closer,

we can sip through our wooden,
tubal tongues the most ancient of grammars—
and although the dance will be hidden from us,
we can follow along through the piping.

The Warboys Journal: Two

Virginia Woolf at Seventeen

In a St. Ives second hand book store I purchased LOGICK: OR THE Right Use of REASON WITH A Variety of RULES To Guard Against ERROR in the AFFAIRS of RELIGION and HUMAN LIFE as well as in the Sciences, by the Late Reverend & Learned Isaac Watts D. D. I care nothing for its LOGICK but bought it for its binding & now am pasting over every REASON & RULE my own journal pages. Resplendent, tooled calf imparts such dignity.

§ §

I remain stunned by the flatness of the Fens. Today, from the slight elevation of my bicycle seat I could see the broad ditch that crosses the land for miles, straight as a yard measure. The water it holds is brown & perhaps in winter it slices the Fens like a dark scar. But today that inevitable disfigurement was softened by reeds and a haze of white moths. Pale reeds, white moths—a seam-line dissolving quite beautifully as it stretched away from me.

§ §

My pen is rather unwell at present. I practice my penmanship to rouse it.

Long ago there was some question which I do not now remember. . .

Long ago there. . .

This curiously sensual love of all that is. . .

Long. . .

Long went the days. . .

§ §

I am happy to say that my pages describing a dismal, endless, rain-spattered picnic have covered entirely Watts's chapter on The Origins and Causes of Equivocal Words.

write   wright   right   rite

rein   reign   rain

§ §

Autumn has come to Warboys. There is that mellow clearness in the air, which softens & matures the land & the mens faces who till it.

The woods decay, the woods decay &
fall; the vapours weep their burden to the ground
Man only comes & tills the earth & lies beneath
& after many a summer dies the swan.
This I. . .
This I write in the year of a. . .

§ §

I met a Fen funeral coming back from Warboys, 5 bakers carts & a corn cart, all filled with people dressed in deep mourning. For at least a mile, down a straight white road, their small procession crawled toward me & then passed me in absolute silence to disappear into the heart of the Fens. I dreamt of those people last night & the vast sky above the flatness & the wind blowing blue spaces around the clouds. Today is the 4th of September. This landscape contains such bleakness. Nevertheless I own it is a joy to me to be set for a time upon it.

§ §

"In all your distributions," Dr. Watts tells me, "observe the nature of things with great exactness. . . . to gain a clear and distinct idea of passion. . . ."

Over his words I am now pasting six carts, one long, white road, blue spaces within a cloud-crowded sky, a bit of joy, & a single day in time. How long will it be, I wonder, until the fabric that divides us crumbles & my sentences end what his began?

The nature of things. . . crawled toward me

The Right Use of Reason. . . stretched away from me

Logick. . . was softened by reeds and a haze of white moths

A variety of Rules. . . passed me in absolute silence

Poets of the Somme: A Cento

And have we done with War at last?
The level evening falls
against the western sky
and the first meadow-flowers appear.

What are we doing here?
Brother Lead and Sister Steel,
by wire and wood and stake we're bound,
knit in the webbing of the rifle-thong.

When Spring comes round again this year
upon the shadowy river—
What are we doing here?—
and starlings in a wood,

and smothered ferns,
and white roads vanishing beneath the sky,
by all the glories of the day
we know that these are good:

slim poplars after rain,
unbroken in these ancient fields.

Cento for Sydney

Between the woods and frozen lake,
Above the narrow road through pine barrens,
On the other side of the bridge,

I heard no voice in the heart, just the hum of the wires.
A shadow imperceptibly darkening
Swayed like the slow movement of a hunting bird

Then all the birds of the air
Glittered a bit above the landscape, the hills
Suffused still with a faint retroactive light.

I don't believe that we will be lifted up
                              and transfixed by radiance
But I could not resist the lovely shape
Against the sunlight and the future's glare:

A shadow imperceptibly darkening
Then all the birds of the air,
Their sudden white underwings. I follow

The cold, never letting go of you,
That day and this,
Our leaves and lakes, our woods.

I think from this distance
About things given that are taken away
and given again in another form.

I don't believe in the inextinguishable light
                              of the other world,
But I could not resist the lovely shape,
This lightest of curtains the curve of it shines.

The Hardy Tree

with lines by Thomas Hardy and Alan Turing

1941

An ancient pulse, the young man thought—germ
and birth, germ and birth—then shut the door
on the clicking Bombes, their rhythmic search
for words within a cryptogram, and rode away.
From Bletchley Park to London. Just for an evening,
two hours or three. Just for the time it took
to spiral down from war to. . . what?
Beyond his train, the late-blue, lately fractured sky
quivered. Thin smoke without flame
rose from the couch grass. Everywhere
a brokenness—that this late day
of thought, and pact, and code
still failed to mend.

§ §

Because the poet had stood in the churchyard
and watched, by flare lamps, the graves unearthed,
watched each night the unclaimed bodies
packed away, the graveyard cinch and cinch
its boundaries so—why?—so trains might pass;
because the poet had scanned the sky,
the belfries and steeples, dark against
a paler dark; because he had heard
a fox bark, sonorous and long—
three barks, horn-like
but melancholy,

§ §

the young man wanted the same churchyard,
the same gradually darkening, quiet sky.
Along the railroad berm, sparse clumps of heather
twitched and stilled. Twitched and stilled.
Gritty semaphores. Then he stood in the churchyard
where Hardy once stood. There was the ash tree,
and there—in memoriam perhaps?—
the upright headstones placed in rings
around its trunk. Just three or four
evenly spaced, concentric rings.
But no,

§ §

that was eighty years ago. Now the ash tree's roots
had nudged the rings into a jumbled cluster,
had tipped, in little groups of two and three,
some stones together. One and one
and two and three. Is that a code?
Nature's logarithmic shrug?

§ §

1931
Matter is meaningless, he wrote at eighteen,
in the absence of spirit. Then something about the body
and death. In the deal sheen of public-school classrooms,
everyone wrote of the body and death. Everyone heard
the syllables slide from *leaves* to *war* to *vacancy*,
and touched the words and spoke the sounds
and saw the oxen kneel. No brittle
ciphers yet. Just fluid
mystery.

§ §

1941

Leaves: serrated. Last to open—he had read this
somewhere—first to fall. Blossoms: petalless.
And the dark trunk, eighty years in the ground:
fissured vertically. The seeds are weights
on weightless wings, oval, embedded, forward-thrust—
the whole so unbalanced it spirals down.
The wholes are "keys"—but why? Because
they click? Because their spinning-jenny
whirligigs, between pure flight and gravity,
unlock a little fuse?

§ §

Almost evening. Everywhere a brokenness—and yet
London seemed held by the strangest silence,
like—what were the lines?—like the belfry loft
when the tenor after tolling stops its hum.
A few lights began in the windows. A few blackout curtains
closed. And do we progress, as Hardy wondered,
not in a straight line but a looped orbit, half
doomed to the past as we wheel forward?
There, just above him, was the ash tree.
There, at his feet, the dust of the lark
that Shelley heard.

§ §

1920

Mother, very new boys here must run
through the paddles. I have tried
to predict their rhythm
and will dodge accordingly.

§ §

1941

Had he slept a bit? His own words circling up
from deep in his childhood? A fountain pen, Mother,
of my own invention   a typewriter
of my own invention   slide along
to the round *A*   press
down

§ §

Then a stirring began in the ash tree, just under
the keys. Finches perhaps? Or nightingales? Thrush?
And over the churchyard came the thrum of engines
in the black cars and the long horn—he loved the sound—
of an inbound train crossing the field behind him.
Was it higher than the ash? That stirring? Some dark shape
shifting in from the Channel? But no, it was birds
in the limbs. Nightingales—slide along—finches, thrush.
Young birds—to the round—young birds
that just a year ago were not birds at all,
but only particles of grain,
and earth, and air, and rain.

Notes on the Centones

"Self-Portrait: A Cento": lines and phrases by Peter Meinke, Dan Beachy-Quick, Ayi Kwei Armah, Emily Grosholz, William Shakespeare, Davis McCombs, James Richardson, Malachi Black, Amy Uyematsu, Jean Valentine, Zach Savich

"Wartime Domicilium: A Cento": lines and phrases by Thomas Hardy, Vladimir Nabokov, Rupert Brooke

"Lepidopteran: A Cento": lines and phrases by Vladimir Nabokov, Thomas Hardy, Alan Turing

"Poets of the Somme: A Cento": lines by Robert Graves, William Noel Hodgson, Alan Seeger, Wilfred Owen, Siegfried Sassoon

"Cento for Sydney": lines by Robert Frost, Norman Dubie, James Wright, Robert Penn Warren, W.S. Merwin, Robert Hass, Louise Glück, Edward Hirsch, Daniel Hoffman, Richard Wilbur, Gjertrud Schnackenberg, Philip Levine, Jean Garrigue, Jorie Graham, Stanley Moss, Linda Gregerson

Acknowledgments

Grateful acknowledgment is made to the following publications where these poems first appeared, some in slightly earlier forms:

Aperçus: "Nabokov's Colored Hearing," "Poets of the Somme," "Self-Portrait, 2016: A Fusion"

Arkansas International: "Identity Matrix," "Lessons of the War: Deviant Identity Formations," "On the Somme"

The Atlantic: "Encryption"

Blackbird: "The Warboys Journal: One," "The Warboys Journal: Two"

Kenyon Review: "Ivory Tightrope Walker"

Narrative: "The Christmas Truce: 1914," "Marking the Swans," "Wartime Domicilium"

New England Review: "The Hardy Tree"

Plume: "The Bird Trap," "Bone Cockerel," "Color: An Elegy," "Magna Carta: An Embroidery," "Magna Carta: An Erosion"

Poem-a-Day (Academy of American Poets): "Evolution," "Lunar Eclipse," "Metamorphosis: 1680"

Poetry: "Lepidopteran: A Cento," "The Underwings of War"

Poetry Northwest: "Camouflage," "Silk Hall: Sherborne School, 1929"

Smithsonian: "Secure Speech Cipher System"

WA129: "The Hive at Kew Gardens"

"Camouflage" also appeared in *Poetry Daily,* 23 July 2018

Italicized lines in "Evolution" are paraphrases of Erwin Schrödinger's words in *What is Life?*

About the Author

Linda Bierds is the author of nine previous poetry collections, the most recent of which, *Roget's Illusion,* was long-listed for the 2014 National Book Award. Her poems have appeared in such magazines as *The Atlantic, The New Yorker, Smithsonian,* and *Poetry,* and she has received numerous awards, including fellowships from the MacArthur Foundation, the Guggenheim Memorial Foundation, and twice from the National Endowment for the Arts. She is the Grace M. Pollock Professor of Creative Writing at the University of Washington in Seattle and lives on Bainbridge Island.

Poetry is vital to language and living. Since 1972, Copper Canyon Press has published extraordinary poetry from around the world to engage the imaginations and intellects of readers, writers, booksellers, librarians, teachers, students, and donors.

WE ARE GRATEFUL FOR THE MAJOR SUPPORT PROVIDED BY:

THE PAUL G. ALLEN
FAMILY FOUNDATION

The Chinese character for poetry is made up of two parts:
"word" and "temple." It also serves as pressmark for
Copper Canyon Press.

The poems are set in Minion Pro.
Book design and composition by Phil Kovacevich.